AUTHOR

Paolo Crippa (23 April 1978) has cultivated his passion for Italian history since high school. His research interests are focused mainly in the field of military history and in particular on italian armored units from the 30s until the end of World War II. In 2006 he published his first volume, "I Reparti Corazzati della Repubblica Sociale Italiana 1943/1945", the first organic research carried out and published in Italy on the subject. In 2007 he published "Duecento Volti della R.S.I." and in 2011 " Un anno con il 27° Reggimento Artiglieria Legnano". He regularly contributes to several journals: Milites, New Historica, SGM - World War II, Batailes & Blindes, Armoured Vehicles and history of the twentieth century, Mezzi Corazzati, both as an author, or in collaboration with other researchers. He published with the editor Mattioli 1885 in 2014 "Italy 43 – 45 – Civil War improvised AFV's" (2014), "Italian AFV's of the Civil War 1943 - 1945" (2015) and "Italy 43 – 45 – AFV's and MV's of co-belligerent units" (2018).

PUBLISHING'S NOTES

None of unpublished images or text of our book may be reproduced in any format without the expressed written permission of Luca Cristini Editore (already Soldiershop.com) when not indicate as marked with license creative commons 3.0 or 4.0. Luca Cristini Editore has made every reasonable effort to locate, contact and acknowledge rights holders and to correctly apply terms and conditions to Content.

Every effort has been made to trace the copyright of all the photographs. If there are unintentional omissions, please contact the publisher in writing at: info@soldiershop.com, who will correct all subsequent editions.

Our trademark: Luca Cristini Editore©, and the names of our series & brand: Soldiershop, Witness to war, Museum book, Bookmoon, Soldiers&Weapons, Battlefield, War in colour, Historical Biographies, Darwin's view, Fabula, Altrastoria, Italia Storica Ebook, Witness To History, Soldiers, Weapons & Uniforms, Storia etc. are herein © by Luca Cristini Editore.

LICENSES COMMONS

This book may utilize part of material marked with license creative commons 3.0 or 4.0 (CC BY 4.0), (CC BY-ND 4.0), (CC BY-SA 4.0) or (CC0 1.0). We give appropriate attribution credit and indicate if change were made in the acknowledgments field. Our WTW books series utilize only fonts licensed under the SIL Open Font License or other free use license.

For a complete list of Soldiershop titles please contact Luca Cristini Editore on our website: www.soldiershop.com or www.cristinieditore.com. E-mail: info@soldiershop.com

Title: **ITALIAN ARMOURED UNITS IN FRANCE DURING THE SECOND WORLD WAR**
Code.: **WTW-062 EN** by Paolo Crippa
ISBN code: 9791255890928 first edition September 2024
Language: English, size: 177,8x254mm Cover & Art Design: Luca S. Cristini

WITNESS TO WAR (SOLDIERSHOP) is a trademark of Luca Cristini Editore, via Orio, 33/D - 24050 Zanica (BG) ITALY.

WITNESS TO WAR

ITALIAN ARMOURED UNITS IN FRANCE DURING THE SECOND WORLD WAR

PHOTOS & IMAGES FROM WORLD WARTIME ARCHIVES

PAOLO CRIPPA

BOOKS TO COLLECT

CONTENTS

Introduction...5

Western Front (June 1940)...7
    Armoured units...9
        1st Tank Infantry Regiment..9
        3rd Tank Infantry Regiment..12
        33rd Tank Infantry Regiment..12
        Frontier Guard - Tankers Companies...13
        Considerations on the use of tanks during the Battle of the Alps........................15

Occupation of Southern France (November 1942 - September 1943)........................49
    Armoured units...50
        II Armoured Squadron Group 'San Marco'...50
        Piedmont Royal Cavalry Regiment...51
        18th Armoured Bersaglieri Regiment..51
        224th Coastal Division..54

Occupation of Corsica (November 1942 - September 1943).....................................63
    Armoured units...65
        CXXXI Battalion Semoventi da 47/32 of Infantry Division 'Cremona'.......65
        XX Self-propelled 47/32 Battalion of the 'Friuli' Infantry Division.............65
        I Tank Battalion L of the 33rd Tank Regiment...65
        II Tank Battalion L of the 33rd Tank Regiment..66
        XIII Tank Battalion L of the 33rd Tank Regiment..66
        10th Celere Regiment..66

Bibliography..97

INTRODUCTION

During the Second World War, the contribution of the Regio Esercito's armoured units on the French front was quite marginal and, for this reason, never examined organically. The deployment of tanks in the first days of the conflict in the Alps, however, should have offered important food for thought for the Italian Commands, because serious difficulties were immediately apparent both in the deployment of the tanks employed, which proved to be totally inadequate, and in the tactics of armoured units, signs that were completely ignored and that caused the same errors to permeate the subsequent phases of the conflict. After this early interlude, armoured units were only sent to France in November 1942, to garrison the coasts of southern France and Corsica, precisely with the task of garrisoning an occupied country and, consequently, never deployed in combat. The Armistice of 8 September 1943, however, marked a turning point: while the units deployed in southern France did not take part in any fighting and returned to Italy, the armoured units stationed in Corsica reacted to German attempts to seize key points on the island and engaged in long days of fighting against the former Allies, fighting that ended with the Germans abandoning Corsica.

▲ L3 Flamethrower Tank Column of the 4th Battalion 'Monti' of the 1st Infantry Regiment on the move out of Susa, towards the Moncenisio Highway (Benvenuti - Colonna).

▲ A Carrista lieutenant, leaning on his L3/35 Radio tank, holds a small dog in his arms. The photograph was taken in Val Stretta, in the Bardonecchia area, in June 1940.

WESTERN FRONT (JUNE 1940)

For Italy, 10 June 1940 marked the beginning of the tragedy of the Second World War: the declaration of war on France and Great Britain triggered hostilities and, as an immediate effect, also an attack on the Alpine front against France, an enemy by then already bent by the much more powerful German attack, which had invested the transalpine country from the north and east. The so-called 'Battle of the Western Alps' was a very short campaign for Italy, declared on 10 June itself, just after the entry into the war on Germany's side, and ended with the armistice of 25 June, but practically only four days of actual fighting (21 to 24 June). This operational cycle forced the Italian Armed Forces to abruptly switch from a purely defensive to an offensive[1] type of deployment and brought Italy only skimpy territorial gains, but it highlighted a substantial Italian strategic failure, which was not, however, unfortunately interpreted as a general alarm signal by the Italian Commands. In fact, the campaign highlighted a series of errors in its approach (lack of good commanders at all levels, scarce synergy between the units engaged at the front, almost non-existent logistics) and the limitations of the military apparatus (poor armaments, lack of vehicles, outdated equipment and clothing unsuitable for combat in difficult areas), but, as had already happened at the end of the Spanish Civil War, the lesson learnt was of no use and the same errors and shortcomings were repeated for the entire duration of the conflict.

Based on a calculation that turned out to be completely wrong, Mussolini counted on the fact that the French armed forces were close to collapse, comforted also by intelligence reports that, although they had correctly assessed the inferior size of the French forces compared to the Italian ones (6 Divisions against 21 Italian ones[2]), they had underestimated the 'rage' factor. The French were not entirely resigned to defeat and, aided by the impervious terrain and a decent system of border fortifications, unleashed a virulent counter-attack against the Italian troops. The Royal Army deployed two Armies in the Western Alps, the 4th Army in the north (from the Swiss border to Mount Granero, north of Monviso, commanded by General Alfredo Guzzoni) and the 1st Army in the south from Mount Granero to the Ligurian Sea, commanded by General Alfredo Pintor)[3], while the French had at their disposal the Armée des Alpes (General René - Henri Orly), which consisted of 2 Corps of

---

[1] At the beginning of June, Marshal Badoglio, Chief of the General Staff, in the course of a meeting with the Chiefs of Staff of all the Armed Forces, had communicated the Duce's strategy: 'The strategy on the fronts must be based on the strictest defensive approach on the ground and in the air. The armed forces, especially the army and air force, must be reserved for the future. On the Western Alps front, therefore, it is advisable to refrain from taking any initiatives'. (from 'June 1940 - War in the Alps', page 63, work cited in bibliography).

[2] The fact that, despite the large number of Divisions engaged, the results of the attack on France were very poor is explained by the belief held by the Italian high command that true strength lay in the quantity of mobilisable units and not in their quality. As a consequence, the Italian Divisions were weak in terms of personnel (binary structure), with dismounted infantry, artillery almost exclusively animal-drawn, and very few armoured components, according to a configuration that made them resemble the large units of the First World War and therefore completely unsuited to a concept of warfare that, in the meantime, had evolved and modernised. Not least, it is important to emphasise that of 73 Divisions, efficient on paper, there were only 19 that were actually complete.

[3] During the hostilities, the 7th Army, under the command of His Royal Highness the Duke of Pistoia, Filiberto di Savoia - Genoa, was deployed in tactical reserve in the area between Acqui and Asti in Piedmont.

Armies, the 14th (General Beynet) and the 15th (General Montagne), as well as 80 Sections Eclaireurs Skieurs (Platoons of ski scouts); the Armée des Alpes was barricaded in the so-called 'Maginot of the Alps', a system of static defences that, although not very modern, could in fact offer the attackers a hard time, also thanks to the orography of the territory. Based on this error of judgement, Mussolini gave the order for the offensive on the afternoon of 20 June, which was unleashed at dawn; on 24 June, what was essentially the last day of the battle in the Alps, the French line of defence was practically intact, so much so that the front line had suffered minor damage. The Italian plan of attack was to advance the 4th Army (then north of the Italian line) in three directions:

- first route along the St. Bernard roadway, which was to open an outlet in Val d'Isere, with Saez as its target;
- second route between Moncenisio and Frejus, through the Arc Valley;
- first route along Montgenèvre and Val Pellice.

To the south, on the other hand, the 1st Army had to break through the border via Monviso, the Colle della Maddalena, the Col di Tenda and the Cornice carriageway on the Côte d'Azur, in the direction of Marseilles. This fragmentation of the attack front along different routes was due to the fact that, in order to penetrate French territory, given the presence of the mountains, it was necessary to proceed along the carriageable roads that crossed the border, and there were only five of these (Picolo San Bernardo, Moncenisio, Monginevro, Colle della Maddalena, Col di Tenda and Cornice, on the Riviera between Liguria and the Côte d'Azur); A further element of difficulty was represented by the lack of connection between these routes (there were in fact no routes parallel to the border line, which could allow the rapid movement of troops from one line of attack to the other, in case of need) and therefore the routes proceeded independently of each other, creating obvious problems for the attacking troops.

We will not go into further detail on the operations on the French front, which can be analysed in other texts, but will instead examine in detail the events that had the Royal Army's tank units as protagonists in the following paragraphs.

Hostilities officially ended on 25 June 1940, with the Armistice, signed by the French authorities at Villa Incisa, with Italy[4]. As shown by a document drawn up on 21 June by the French ambassador Leon Noël, representative of the transalpine government, the French authorities were against signing an armistice with the Kingdom of Italy, believing in fact that they had not fought any war, but had only sustained minor skirmishes against the Italians and that, consequently, Italy had not won any conflict.

The bill paid by Italy, in terms of human losses, was however high. There were 631 soldiers who had lost their lives, 616 were missing, 2,631 had been wounded or had suffered frostbite injuries (mainly due to clothing and footwear unsuitable for high temperatures). The French troops took 1,141 prisoners after the signing of the armistice; on the other hand,

---

[4] Noël's document even states: *'Italy declared war on us but did not do so. We have no need of an armistice with that country because the mere declaration of war is not war. If we were faced with unacceptable demands in Rome, the whole edifice of our agreement with Germany would collapse. In that case we would not only refuse to sign the document with Italy, but would feel authorised to resume our freedom of action entirely'.* (from 'June 1940 - War on the Alps', page 120, work cited in bibliography).

155 French soldiers had been taken who, instead of being released, were concentrated at the Fonte d'Amore camp. French losses were much more limited: 20 dead (in a frightening ratio of 1 to 30, compared to Italian casualties), 150 missing and 84 wounded[5].

If on the one hand, with the peace agreement, Italy obtained only slight territorial conquests, so much so that they could be defined as 'encroachments of a few kilometres,' on the other hand, the end of hostilities decreed the disappearance of the Regia Marina's then main adversary in the Mediterranean: the French fleet.

Armoured Units

1st Tank Infantry Regiment

The Regiment, which was based in Vercelli, was mobilised in June 1940 and formed the 4th Army's Celere Regiment, together with the 4th Bersaglieri Regiment and the Nizza Cavalry Regiment (1st). The Regiment took part in operations on the French front with its Battalions I, II and IV:

- I Tank Battalion L 3/35 *'Major Ribet'*.
- II Tank Battalion L 3/35 *'General Berardi'*
- IV Tank Battalion L 3/35 *'General Monti'*

His 3rd Tank Battalion, equipped with the now antiquated L 5/30, better known as FIAT 3000, did not take part in the operations on the Alpine Front.

At the end of the operations in France, the Regiment was first sent to Fiume and later to North Africa.

The 4th 'Monti' Tank Battalion took part in the fighting in the Moncenisio area, reinforcing Alpine and Infantry units[6]. The 1st Company arrived in Aosta in the evening of 22 June and was made to continue, during the night, along the Arc valley to the Moncenisio pass. After passing the barrage of two French forts and crossing the border, the Battalion's tanks easily overran a first enemy barrage, went around a bridge and encountered a second barrage. Here the 1st Company commander's tank jumped over a mine and a second armoured tank met the same end while trying to recover the first tank. The mine field was blown up with a hand grenade and the tanks were thus able to continue their march to the bottom of the valley, occupying a village. Between 23 and 24 June, the French defensive positions, which controlled the RN 6 road, prevented the 'Monti' Battalion and the first divisions of the 'Trento' Motorised Division from moving down into the valley. Although the four 149/35 pieces from Fort Paradiso on the Moncenisio intervened by striking the French positions, the 5th Tank Battalion and the 'Trento' Division were unable to provide any concrete help to the I Corps forces in the Val d'Arc (specifically, the 4th Tank Battalion was supposed to

---

5 Achille Starace's judgement on the campaign against France was inclement: *'Men were sent to a useless death with the same systems as twenty years ago'.* (from 'June 1940 - War on the Alps', page 128, work cited in bibliography).

6 The 4th Assault Tank Battalion 'Monti', stationed in Bolzano, had been transferred from the 2nd Carrista Infantry Regiment in Verona to the 1st Carrista Infantry Regiment in Vercelli in November 1938. It was later transferred to the newly formed 32nd Carrista Infantry Regiment (which was nothing more than the new name of the 2nd Regiment); according to some sources, the 'Monti' was assigned to the 32nd Regiment in 1939, but in fact took part in operations on the French Front as part of the 1st Regiment.

support the 'Brenner' Division). The coming of the 'cease-fire' on the 25th marked the end of the offensive movement of the 'Monti' Battalion. The 5th Company of the 4th Battalion of the 1st Regiment, equipped with L3/35 flamethrower tanks, took part in the operation that led to the conquest of the fort Ouillon des Arcellins, at an altitude of 2,665 metres, carried out by a battalion of the "Cagliari" Infantry Division, two platoons of the 2nd Company "Lupi del Moncesio" and a company of the 4th Bersaglieri Regiment, mobilised as a reserve. During the operations, the 4th Assault Tank Battalion 'Monti' had 7 casualties and its members were decorated with 3 Silver Military Valour Medals and 1 Bronze Military Valour Memorial Medal.

In his diary, Carrista sergeant Domenico Fossati summarises the events that occurred on the French Front with the 1st Carrista Infantry Regiment:

"Two days after leaving for Susa, our front sector will be the Moncenisio. Susa is packed with soldiers. I learn that there have been some rather serious brawls between Alpine soldiers and black shirts over the possession of barracks which, so they say, had been prepared for the Army and not for the Militia. Here in Susa we listen to the Duce's speech that ends with that word: We will win, and immediately afterwards we leave for our sector. I don't want to be controversial but only imbeciles could think of deploying tanks on rocky terrain, immense pine forests, with only one road at an altitude of almost two thousand metres. We set up camp near the lake not far from the refuge hotel, which, although Italian, is regularly looted. Ferrero and Sella manage to procure a more than respectable reserve of wine, which is, of course, distributed among the members of the old 'association' formed in Vercelli. It snows continuously.

As it was 10 June, we were already wearing canvas fatigue trousers. The Italian army had no anti-freeze for the radiators so we had to lie under the tanks every evening in the slush mixed with sleet to empty the radiators and then fill them again the next morning. Not even a shadow of the French, at least in our sector, but we know that there have already been clashes between alpine and bersaglieri on one side and chasseur des Alpes on the other. There is also talk of cases of frostbite, but fortunately not in our departments. We manage to defend ourselves from the cold better than others because instead of pitching tents in the snow, we have turned our SPA38 and Dovunque into small dormitories. We are packed in like chickens, but at least not in contact with the ground. General V., commander of the entire sector, has arrived at Mont-Cenis. In the previous days, we were visited by the Prince of Piedmont, commander of the Army of the Po.

The beginning of what we could call the offensive has something unreal about it, I cannot believe my eyes. We are lined up near the lake, the 'Monti' battalion in the lead, ours in the rear. General V. delivers a speech as vacuous as it is rhetorical. The terrain before us is absolutely impassable to our means. The only route that can allow us to cross the border is the Mont Cenis road. To think that this only access route has not been mined is simply demented, yet no one seems to realise this. Where the French are I do not know, but they are certainly watching us from their posts. We are standing there beside our tanks waiting for I don't know what. Not a single unit is deflected from the more than likely enemy fire. I'm wondering why they haven't opened fire on such a tempting immovable target yet. Perhaps they too are hesitant to start such a stupid and senseless war. These and a thousand other thoughts pass through my mind as I watch, spectator-actor to this carnival that only because of the French has not yet turned into a massacre. A few well-aimed salvos on our magnificent deployment of platoons well flanked and lined up and the first tank regiment would have come to an end. I was so convinced that I would not reach the end of the day that as I began my second packet of milit I had already drained my ration of cognac, which was part of the emergency supplies, for which there was a strict instruction not to touch them without a higher order.

Finally, General V. makes a decision. Without consulting either the regimental or battalion commander, he directly gives the order to the first tank that is close by: 'Engines ahead'. The unfortunate man has no choice but to obey, start the engine and set off on the road across the border, he advances for about two hundred metres, then predictably runs into a mine and for the two tank drivers, the war ends before it begins. I feel like crying so much it's absurd. I look at my men, they are simply dumbfounded, one is vomiting. The undaunted general orders the second tank to advance.

The French continue to hold their fire. The second tank, albeit with less boldness, starts up and advances, after about two hundred metres it follows the fate of the first. Screams are heard, evidently the driver or tank leader is still alive, but nothing moves.

The general orders the third tank to advance. At this point, as if by the breaking of an evil spell, the major commander of the "Monti" stops the tank that was already moving forward and standing at attention in front of the general says: "Your Excellency, this time we will go, I will be the pilot and you will be the leader of the tank". There is a dead silence, the general first mumbles something unintelligible then adds: 'we will talk about it'. He gets into his car and drives off towards Susa. Such is the rage and hatred in me at such a spectacle of incompetence and cowardice that without any order I leap onto my tank and go to try to bring help to the second tank, the one from which groans are rising. I try to follow his lead and when I am three or four metres behind him I leap out and with the cable catch him in tow. My fear is only that he has the gear jammed or that my tank is unable to tow him. At that moment the French open fire with their artillery. Evidently they were already on target because the shots fell very close. Fortunately for me they were not the first ones I heard, I quickly hook the cable and attempt to throw myself into the tank. At that precise moment a grenade bursts very close to me and I feel a great heat in my leg, I was hit by some shrapnel. Now I can't get out any more, I couldn't walk, and to stay there means to die, unfortunately the leg that was hit is the one I need for the accelerator, go as you wish I have to try to make it, the cable stretches and I start to fall back. The hit tank follows me, the French no longer fire. I reach our deployment, my mind is numb, I'm losing a lot of blood, I hear Lieutenant Catherine's voice in the distance shouting something like: "who gave you the order, we'll talk about it. But I don't seem to detect any animosity in his tone.

My good friend Ferrero says to me as they lay me on the ground in the snow: 'Always lucky, Grandpa, for you the war is over!' Finally an ambulance arrives and I am loaded with other wounded and sent first to Susa then to Turin.

Twenty days later I was discharged from hospital; then came the news of the proposed war cross for valour, the appointment as sergeant major and a week of arrest for carrying out an operation without having received the order".

---

[7] Taken from 'Diario di un sergente della Fanteria Carrista', by Giorgio Corino, which appeared in 'Il Carrista d'Italia', magazine of the Associazione Nazionale Carristi d'Italia.

3rd Tank Infantry Regiment

The 3rd Bologna Carristi Regiment deployed the 5th and 11th Battalions, both equipped with L3/35 tanks, on the French front from the beginning of hostilities, as part of the 1st Army's Celere Regiment, but did not take part in any major operations. At the end of the operations in France, the Regiment returned to its headquarters in Bologna.

33rd Tank Infantry Regiment

After the declaration of war, the 33rd Carristi Regiment of the 'Littorio' Division was the first armoured unit to be operationally deployed. The Regiment, which was commanded by Colonel De Lorenzis, consisted of 4 L Tank Battalions, the only undivided battalions, which participated in the campaign on the French front. The Regiment was transferred to the Aosta area from 19 June, with the aim of breaking through the French defences on the western front in the Little St. Bernard area.

The transfer of the units took place by rail on various convoys and the first unit to arrive in the area of operations on 22 June was the 1st Tank Battalion L. It was sent from the Aosta railway station towards the French-Italian border along the roadway leading to Piccolo San Bernardo, to make itself available to the 'Trieste' Motorised Division. The Battalion reached the border area at dawn on 23 June, with orders to head for the town of Saez, following an attack route that was to open an outlet into the Isère valley. The march was made difficult by the cannon fire from the French fort of Traversette and by the conditions of the terrain, made impassable by the bad weather (there had even been heavy snowfall) and, for this reason, the tanks advanced in single file along the asphalt strip of the road, offering themselves as easy targets for possible enemy attacks, which were not long in coming and it is not surprising that on that very first day of attack, a small tragedy occurred for the tanks. In fact, at around 7 a.m., after having passed through a first barricade at an altitude of almost 2,000 metres, just before the hairpin bends that descend to Saez, the column ran into a second road barrier, this one mined with detonating devices tied directly to the barbed wire fences, and the leading tank blew up, blocking the advance of the rest of the column, which remained exposed to the French artillery fire, and two other tanks were dislodged, having become entangled in the barbed wire. The column managed to disengage and reverse, only at the cost of abandoning the stricken tank and its crew, consisting of Lieutenant Carlo Montecchi and Corporal Rosario De Vita. Given the obvious impossibility of breaking through the French resistance, backed up by fire from the fort of Traversette, the I Tank Battalion L was withdrawn in the evening of the same day and a rescue team was sent to recover the hit tank in the morning. During the recovery operations, the radio tank of Lieutenant Vincenzo Giummolè, the Battalion's adjutant, jumped on a mine and the officer died shortly after being transported in a very serious condition to the dressing station, located in the San Bernardo hospice, where the bodies of Lieutenant Montecchi and Corporal De Vita had also been transferred, who was found still alive, but died shortly after his recovery. Lieutenant Giummolè, Lieutenant Montecchi and Corporal De Vita were all awarded the Silver Military Valour Medal of Remembrance; Sergeant Attilio Polise was also decorated with the Bronze Military Valour Medal of Remembrance, and Second Lieutenant Vittorio Pennacchioni with the Silver Military Valour Medal.

This is the recollection of the Alpine campaign by Carrista Oliviero Cervi, of the 2nd Battalion of the 33rd Carristi Regiment, taken from his memoirs[8]:

"*We are at the camp, in full training fervour when, on the tenth of June '40, we are assembled in front of the radio to listen to the declaration of war. In truth, they are not much in the way of unbridled enthusiasm and the euphoria of some is quite fleeting: but neither is there any hint of dissent or protest.*

A week has passed and here is the order to leave for the 'western front': we are suddenly convinced that we have to change our persuasions and habits; from now on, bullets will no longer be harmless; adversaries will no longer be other tank drivers from the battalion, but unknown enemies who will not hesitate, with powerful and deadly weapons, to oppose our advance. Be that as it may, one fact is certain: nobody 'asks for a visit' or clings to futile pretexts to ambush.

Departure at the crack of dawn: all night in the slow, unlit carriage and arrival early in the morning in Aosta; the camp is established just outside the town.

Strange, uncontrollable, exhilarating or depressing news is circulating among the troops: we deliberately ignore it. Everyone looks after the specific tasks entrusted to them and with justifiable impatience awaits the moment of the tussle.

To cross the demarcation line, the 1st battalion, employed suddenly, adventurously, almost on the eve of the armistice, goes up: the small L/3, which become tiny in the face of the majesty of the mountains, are thrown to the mercy of the enemy. Officers, non-commissioned officers and tank men fall dead or wounded: it is the first tribute of blood that will ennoble the blazon of the young regiment.

In the quagmire of flooded meadows, the troops are reviewed by Prince Umberto. Perhaps, who knows, it may be that amidst the sudden flare-up of exaltation due to the presence of the young commander of the western army group, there are also those who judge severely the conduct of the war in the Alps. Perhaps, I say'.

In July 1940, the Regiment was returned to its headquarters in Parma, where it was reviewed by Benito Mussolini.

Frontier Guard - Comrade Tankers

By the end of January 1940, five Tanker Companies had been created as part of the Frontier Guard, equipped with about fifty old FIAT 3000 tanks, both model 21 and model 30 (at the time classified as L5/21 and L5/30 light tanks), taken from the Carristi divisions of the Regio Esercito already existing on national territory and not mobilised; each Company was organised on a radio-controlled tank and three Plotons on three tanks each. In addition, 2 heavy trucks, 2 carts, 1 light truck, 1 car, 2 motorbikes, with a staff of 4 officers, 5 non-commissioned officers and 35 tank drivers completed the equipment.

The 2nd, 4th and 5th G.A.F. Tank Companies took part in the campaign against France:

- **2nd Company**: based in Borgo San Dalmazio (CN), commanded by Lieutenant Costantino Marchi, assigned to the 3rd Covering Sector. At the end of May 1940 it passed to the 2nd Army Corps of the 1st Army; during the offensive against France it

---

[8] "The II/33rd, my battalion", typewritten memoir, cited in the bibliography.

was stationed in the Vinadio area, on the road leading to the Colle della Maddalena (Magdalen Pass), without moving or taking part in any action.

- **4th Company:** commanded by Lieutenant Adone Visconti, it was part of the 7th Cover Sector, responsible for the defence of Mont Cenis. At the beginning of the war, it was attached to the 4th Army Corps. It was stationed in Cesana Torinese (TO), on State Road No. 24 of Montgenèvre, an important pass with France, but, once the conflict began, it was placed under the "Sforzesca" Division, which had the task of forcing the French defences in the Briançon basin. On the evening of 17th June, the Company received orders to converge on Clavière and the transfer began the following morning, but the hairpin bends that climbed up to Fort Chaberton were too steep and the tanks were unable to cover the short distance, getting stuck and having to return to Cesana. The mechanics of the unit managed to restore three tanks to efficiency, with which a Platoon was formed, which only managed to reach Clavière on 21 June, with great difficulty. Around noon on 22nd June, the Italian Command gave the order to occupy the small village of Mont Genèvre and the operation was carried out by a Platoon of formation of the Carabinieri Company of Montgenèvre, supported by the 3 FIAT 3000 tanks of the 4th Carristi Company of the G.A.F.: the Carabinieri penetrated into the town, advancing behind the tanks, which protected them from the French fortification located west of the town. This was the only known war operation in which the L5 tanks (the new name given to the FIAT 3000, according to the regulations that came into force for Italian tanks) of the Guardia Alla Frontiera took part. At the end of the war operations, the Company was returned to the Depot, leaving the dependence on the IV Army Corps and the VII G.A.F. Sector, in order to allow a complete overhaul and refurbishment of the department's tanks.

- **5th Company:** was commanded by Captain Giuseppe Ponzini and at the beginning of May 1940 moved from Riva del Garda to Vallecrosia (IM), in the deployment of the 1st Covering Sector and was the unit with tanks in the best condition. At the beginning of the war, it was included in the XV Army Corps of the 1st Army and was placed under the "Cosseria" Division and was ordered to defend the town of Ventimiglia (IM), with 5 tanks placed in the western part of the town, covering the Via Aurelia, and the other 5 in reserve in the eastern periphery, with Captain Ponzini. The company remained in this position even when the "Cosseria" went on the attack, penetrating French territory, and when hostilities ended, the unit returned to Vallecrosia.

The FIAT 3000 tanks were therefore unable to make a fundamental contribution to the war effort, not only because the planned 'war in the mountains' did not take place on a large scale, as had been planned, but also because of the technological limits that these tanks were now demonstrating, being outdated in modern warfare. On the other hand, it must be remembered, however, that on the same front, the French army exclusively deployed the

Renault FT tanks,[9] elder brothers of the FIAT 3000 (which were in fact a reworked copy of the FT), demonstrating how little use the use of modern tanks in a high-altitude war was considered to be.

At the end of the campaign against France, the 3 Companies were redeployed on the border with Yugoslavia.

Considerations on the use of tanks during the Battle of the Alps

Let us now summarise a number of considerations, which can be drawn from observing the employment of Italian tank divisions during the Battle of the Alps. The operation, although small in scale, proved to be fraught with pitfalls for the Italian armoured units, which from the very beginning of the campaign found themselves operating amidst serious difficulties. The French had made the passes very dangerous, fortifying them skilfully and having them manned by very fierce troops; the access roads, especially on the French side, were excessively steep and made impracticable by the bad weather for the Italian tanks, which found themselves having to proceed using the road system, on which the adversaries had created mine barriers, thus being exposed to the double danger of mines and enemy artillery shots.

The light tanks, which were supposed to form the backbone of Italian combined operations, proved to be completely ineffective against fixed positions, as they were not supported by prior artillery fire: the Battle of the Alps served to dispel the myth of the 'mountain tank', the idea behind the L3 tank concept.

The campaign, therefore, despite being very short in terms of time, demonstrated a certain amount of improvisation (also on the part of the tank officers who, on several occasions, found themselves unprepared as to what to do) and the obsolescence of the light tanks, which were supposed to form the backbone of the armoured units of the Regio Esercito. These tanks, in fact, could not hold their own against fortified works and their use in such contexts was absolutely useless, even in the face of heavy losses.

---

9 These were the tanks of the BCTC, Bataillon de chars des troupes coloniales.

▲ L3/35 flamethrower tanks at the French border (Benvenuti - Colonna).

▼ An L3/35 tank at the Moncenisio Pass (Benvenuti - Colonna).

▲ A column of L3 flamethrower tanks of the 'Littorio' Division ascends from Aosta, heading towards France (Benvenuti - Colonna).

▲ After crossing the border, this column of L3s began to descend towards the valley. The L-tanks had to march in single file on the roadway, easily exposing themselves to enemy fire, as the terrain was impassable due to adverse weather conditions (Benvenuti - Colonna).

▼ An L3/35 tank, probably from the 4th Tank Battalion 'Monti', destroyed by French fire (Benvenuti - Colonna).

▲ During the very brief operations on the Alpine front, some light tanks were lost; the one pictured is Lieutenant Giummolè's tank (Benvenuti - Colonna).

▼ Close-up image of Lieutenant Giummolè's L3/33 Radio tank (registration RE 1761), which exploded on a mine, while attempting to recover the light tank of Lieutenant Montecchi and Corporal De Vita (Benvenuti - Colonna).

▲ A column of Bersaglieri, partly on bicycles, partly transported on Bianchi Mediolanum trucks to Moncenisio.

▼ Tanks marching on the Western Alps front in June 1940: the poor ground conditions can be seen (ACS).

▲ A FIAT 3000 tank, model 21 Radio, without the tail, from a Frontier Guard unit (Benvenuti - Colonna).

▼ One of the few FIAT 3000 tanks, deployed on the Alps front, photographed in Montgenevre (Montgenèvre), after the occupation of the small town (Cucut).

▲ Soldiers during a break in operations on a CL39 light truck (ACS).

▼ Bersaglieri Motorcyclists near Mont Cenis (ACS).

▲ A column of Bersaglieri motorbikes on the valley floor heading towards the Petit St. Bernard (ACS).

▼ Light tank column of the 1st Carrista Infantry Regiment on the Moncenisio plain. At the head of the column is an L3/35, followed by L3/35 Flamethrower (ACS) tanks.

▲ A field workshop in full swing on the Western Front.

▼ Motorised Bersaglieri at a halt near an Alpine pass (ACS).

▲ A CL 39 knocked out by a French artillery shell (ACS).

▼ A L3 flamethrower tank of the 4th Tank Battalion 'Monti' on the march (Cucut).

▲ Infantrymen of the 4th Tank Battalion "Monti" of the 1st Infantry Regiment during a break in operations (Cucut).

▼ Another image of L3 tanks of the 'Monti' Battalion parked at Gran Croce, a hamlet in the municipality of Moncenisio (Cucut).

▲ An L5 tank model 21 (FIAT 3000 tanks were renamed L5 tanks) of the 4th Carristi Company of the Frontier Guard in Cesana (Cucut).

▼ The tanks of the 4th Battalion 'Monti' of the 1st Carrista Infantry Regiment move towards the French border (Cucut).

▲ French soldiers next to two Renault FT17 tanks, in a photograph taken shortly before the war: these were the only tanks deployed by the French on the Alpine front (WEB source).

▼ A motorbike patrol of the Milizia della Strada escorts motorcyclists on their way to the front in the Western Alps in June 1940.

▲ Intense movement of troops of all specialities on the railways near the French-Italian border.

▼ SPA 38 trucks, camouflaged with branches, on the move in the area of the Petit St. Bernard (ACS).

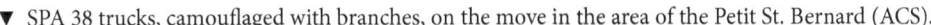

▲ A unit of Bersaglieri motorcyclists ready to advance in the Moncenisio area (ACS).

▼ Artillery units in action on the French border (ACS).

▲ A high-altitude Italian troop contingent.

▲ Infantry soldiers in carts reach the front in the area of the Petit St. Bernard (ACS).

▼ A military photographer at work following operations on the Alpine front (ACS).

▲ Repairing telephone lines in the Petit St Bernard area, in prohibitive weather conditions. A CL39 and an L3 tank (ACS) can be seen.

▼ Motorised troops at the border crossing of the Petit St. Bernard (ACS).

▲ An L3 tank passes a milestone in the Petit St. Bernard area: although it was late June, the Italian troops found themselves operating in an almost wintry environment (ACS).

▼ Italian artillery piece in position (ACS).

▲ Light tank column marching to the Petit St Bernard amidst low clouds (ACS).
▼ An L3/35 flamethrower tank at the St. Bernard (ACS).

▲ The same tank as in the previous photograph, taken from the back. The tank is marked "RE 137 r" (ACS).

▼ French artillery piece captured by Italian troops.

▲ French prisoners.

▼ A tank guards a road junction a few kilometres from Lanslebourg-Mont-Cenis, a French municipality located near the Mont Cenis pass (ACS).

▲ A mortar section passes an L3 tank: the photo was taken in the same spot as the previous one (ACS).
▼ Marching soldiers follow an L3/35 tank to the Mont Cenis pass (ACS).

▲ A large banner on a house in the Western Alps reads: 'WE ARE PASSING AND WE WILL PASS'; the lorries are White Miles (ACS).

▼ A column of light tanks crosses the border of the Petit St. Bernard while a snowstorm rages (ACS).

▲ Road rehabilitation by the Genieri del Regio Esercito of roads blown up by French troops (ACS).

▼ A tank division deployed in the front area (at Moncenisio or Monginevro) on 29 June 1940 awaiting Mussolini's visit (ACS).

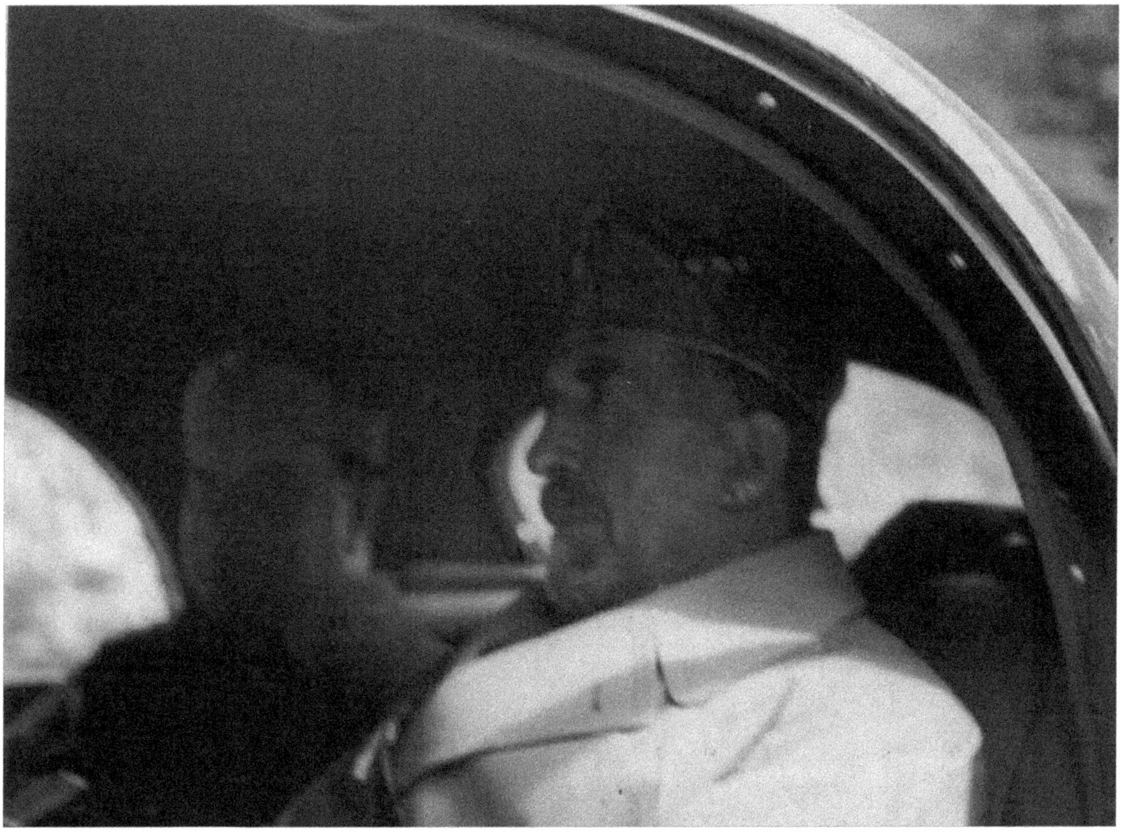

▲ General Alfredo Guzzoni visiting Italian units engaged on the Western Alps front (ACS).

▼ The Italian troops of the 'Trieste' Motorised Division receive a visit from HRH Prince of Piedmont Umberto di Savoia (ACS).

▲ Umberto I reviews a division of Bersaglieri motorcyclists.

▼ Plaque laid in memory of Lieutenants Carlo Montecchi and Vincenzo Giummole and Corporal Rosario Di Vita of the 1st Company of the 33rd Carrier Infantry Regiment of the 'Littorio' Armoured Division, who died during the descent from the Piccolo San Bernardo Pass (ACS).

▲ The tankers of the 33rd Regiment of the 'Littorio' Division, having returned to their headquarters after the campaign on the Western Alps front, are reviewed by Benito Mussolini (Benvenuti - Colonna).

▼ Another image of the tank units of the 33rd Tank Regiment of the 'Littorio' Division being reviewed by Benito Mussolini.

▲ Picture of the Italian-French border before the outbreak of hostilities in June 1940 at the San Luigi bridge at the entrance to Menton. The bar in the photograph is still in existence and functioning today.

▼ Italian heavy artillery in action near Calvo, a hamlet of Ventimiglia: in the background the church of San Pancrazio (ACS).

▲ Effects of the bombardment carried out by the French between 22 and 24 June 1940 on the town of Ventimiglia (ACS).

▼ Italian officers in Ventimiglia on 24 June 1940 (ACS).

▲ Italian trucks destroyed by enemy fire on the Colle della Maddalena (ACS).
▼ An Italian officer points from a panoramic terrace at the town of Menton, which is just across the border.

▲ General Gastone Gambara with some officers in the Ventimiglia area on 24 June 1940 (ACS).
▼ Blackshirts pictured in Menton at the end of clashes with French troops (ACS).

▲ The French delegation goes to Villa Incisa for the signing of the Franco-Italian armistice.

OCCUPATION OF SOUTHERN FRANCE (NOVEMBER 1942 – SEPTEMBER 1943)

The Italian occupation of southern France is a little-studied military event in the overall picture of the Second World War, probably due both to its short duration (apart from a few very small portions close to the borders, such as Menton, it only lasted for about ten months from 1942) and to the total absence of armed resistance events on the part of the local population.

Operation 'Torch', i.e. the Allied landings in Morocco and Algeria, between 8 and 16 November 1942, put the Axis commanders on high alert, who began to perceive (especially the Germans) the territory of 'Vichy France' as a weak link in the southern European defence chain, which could have become a new landing target for the Allies, with which to target the heart of the Old Continent, given also the unreliability of Vichy France's troops demonstrated in North Africa.

For these reasons, the occupation of the territory of Tunisia, which was occupied by the Afrikakorps and the Italian units in North Africa, and the metropolitan areas that made up the so-called Free Zone of France (Operation 'Anton') was planned. The primary objective was the capture of the French fleet in the harbour of Toulon, which still had an interesting war value, and so Operation 'Lila' was planned and implemented, with the aim of seizing as much naval vessels as possible. However, Admiral Jean de Laborde, the French naval commander, managed to negotiate a small truce, thanks to which he was able to smuggle the ships out: the Germans could only watch as the ships sunk themselves off the coast and into the city harbour. The lost navy amounted to 3 battleships, 7 cruisers, 28 destroyers and 20 submarines. The Italians used the remains of the sunken French fleet as casting material.

The Regio Esercito employed a considerable number of resources in Operation 'Anton', the 4th Army and the VII Army Corps. Although the deployment of forces seemed very substantial[10], the Italian units were poorly motorised and the Regio Esercito was not able to occupy all the territory under its jurisdiction, so that the area of occupation was limited: from 12 November, the VII Army Corps occupied Corsica (the events of which we will discuss in the next chapter) while the 4th Army occupied eight south-eastern departments of France (Côte d'Azur, Savoy and even the Principality of Monaco), in an area between the Alpine border, the Rhône River and the Mediterranean coast, excluding the cities of Lyon and Marseilles.

The Italian occupation lasted until the Armistice of 8 September 1943, essentially in a quiet manner, in a framework where the 4th Army, the population, the Vichy government, the Germans (a cumbersome presence) and the Italian Armistice Commission moved. The

---

10 To give a measure of the effort expended in France, it suffices to recall that, according to a report of 31 May 1943, thus in the midst of the occupation of French territory, the 4th Army had 4 Infantry Divisions, 2 Alpine Divisions, 3 Coastal Divisions and other divisions, totalling 6.000 officers and 136,000 non-commissioned officers and troop soldiers, and the VIIth Army Corps had 2 Infantry Divisions, 1 Coastal Division and other divisions, with a total of 3,000 officers and 65,700 non-commissioned officers and troop soldiers.

Italian authorities, in fact, administered the territories in a much less harsh manner than the German ones and the coexistence between the authorities, the local population and the Italian commands, was overall quite peaceful and respectful, favoured by the cultural proximity and the presence of a large Italian community or community of Italian origin, despite the inevitable friction towards the occupiers, the sufficiency and contempt shown by the French population towards an army that in 1940 had not, in fact, defeated them. Italian emigrants, at the time, were generally integrated into French society, but some still found themselves politically linked to Italy, both those who felt close to Fascism (the regime, in fact, supported the annexationist-irredentist aspirations of a stratum of the population) and those in the opposite camp who were emigrants who had escaped because they were opponents of the regime. The opposition of the French population only rarely resulted in real guerrilla actions, in response to which Italian countermeasures were implemented with arrests, trials and internment of Resistance members.

In Nice, the local newspaper 'Il Nizzardo' was re-established and was directed by Ezio Garibaldi, Giuseppe Garibaldi's grandson. Thousands of Jews, including Italian-speaking Jews, had taken refuge in the coastal city, fleeing Nazi persecution, and a number of Jewish organisations were organised there. Thanks to the work of the Jewish lawyer Angelo Donati and the Capuchin friar Father Maria Benedetto, the fascist authorities curbed the application of anti-Semitic laws and the deportation of Jews during the occupation of the city.

Following the landing in Sicily and the events of 25 July 1943, part of the troops stationed in southern France were recalled to Italy; the Germans, fearing an even more negative development of the situation, began preparations for a possible military intervention in the area, an intervention that did not take place until the day after the Armistice. When the Armistice was signed with the Allies, the Germans caught the units of the 4th Army still present in France about to leave: Italian resistance was weak and short-lived; therefore, most of the Italian soldiers were captured; only a few elements managed to go into hiding and join the French Resistance, with great difficulty since they were former occupiers. German troops invaded the areas occupied by the Royal Italian Army and began brutal raids. For its anti-Nazi resistance, Nice was the victim of reprisals and deportations of Jews: in the first 5 years of German occupation, around 5,000 Jews were captured and deported by SS units commanded by Alois Brunner. Brutally bombed by the Allies on 26 May 1944, Nice finally came under Anglo-American control on 28 August, following the Allied landing in the south of France (Operation 'Dragoon').

Armoured Units

II Armoured Squadron Group 'San Marco'

Framed in the 2nd "Emanuele Filiberto Testa di Ferro" Celere Division, it was equipped with L3 and L6 tanks. The Group's units occupied Provence and remained there as an occupation force until September 1943, when, following the Division, it began to move back to its homeland. The 'San Marco' Group was disarmed on its way back to Italy by the Germans.

Piedmont Royal Cavalry Regiment[11]

During the Second World War, the Regiment was part of the 2nd Celere Division 'Emanuele Filiberto Testa di Ferro', with which it took part in the Yugoslavian Campaign in 1941 and later in counter-guerrilla operations in Croatia until 26 June 1942. In the second half of 1942, when the occupation of southern France was planned, the Regiment, which was staffed by the 3rd Group equipped with L6/40 light tanks, followed the fate of the 2nd Celere Division, which began its transfer to occupation territory on 13 November, being deployed first to garrison the Nice area and then along the Menton-Draguignan sector, when it also took control of the Antibes-Saint Tropez coastline. The Piedmont Royal Cavalry Regiment was redeployed for coastal defence and to garrison the towns of Antibes, Théoule, Toulon, Nice, Colle Noire, Tanneron, with the L6/40 Tank Group quartered in the Nice area, patrolling the Antibes-Saint Tropez coastal sector, starting in December, replacing the 58th Infantry Division "Legnano".

The 2nd Celera Division remained in its positions until 4 September 1943, when it began the movement to return home with destination Turin. On 9 September, following the Armistice, the Division initially positioned its units around the city of Turin, to prevent the movement of German troops towards the city, but the following day it moved towards the French border, barricading the Maira and Varaita valleys, to cover the return from France of the Italian units, but was disbanded on 12 September. The Piedmont Royal Cavalry Regiment, having reached Venaria Reale, was placed under the orders of Turin's Territorial Defence Command and was reinforced by a Group of the 134th Artillery Regiment and by units of Bersaglieri cyclists and tank men. Until 12 September, it held out against the German troops, who were aiming at Turin, fighting between Nichelino, Cambiano, Caraglio, Villafalletto and Savigliano. Here, after a charge of the 1st Squadron, near the Savigliano airfield, by superior order, having saved the Standard, the Regiment disbanded on the same 12th September 1943. Having distributed the supplies of food and the little money left in the regimental coffers among the enlisted men, many Knights, who had been left their individual equipment and weapons, managed to overcome the German positions, returning to their homes. Some elements of the Regiment joined the nascent partisan formations, while others were captured by the German armed forces and sent to prison camps in Germany.

18th Armoured Bersaglieri Regiment

The 18th Armoured Bersaglieri Regiment was also sent to southern France. The unit was formed on 1 February 1942 in Siena, at the Depot of the 5th Bersaglieri Regiment, with the personnel based on two battalions, as provided for armoured scout regiments:
- Command
  - Command Platoon and Connections
  - Armoured car platoon

---

11 There is disagreement between the various sources on the name of the unit. Nicola Pignato and Filippo Cappellano maintain that the armoured unit had been named 1st Squadron", but they are not certain about the name "Royal Piedmont". Other sources indicate instead that following the reorganisation of 1 August 1942, the 2nd Celere Division "Emanuele Filiberto Testa di Ferro" received the "Royal Piedmont Cavalry" Regiment, probably the same unit with L6, but with a different name.

- Ferrymen Platoon
- Services Platoon
- LXVIII Armoured Bersaglieri Battalion
  - Command Company
    - Command Platoon and Connections
    - Armoured platoon and reserve tanks
    - Services Platoon
  - 1st Armoured Car Company (out of 17 AB41 armoured cars)
    - Command Platoon
    - 1st Platoon
    - 2nd Platoon
    - 3rd Platoon
    - 4th Platoon
  - 2nd Tank Company L6/40
    - Command Platoon
    - 1st Tank Platoon
    - 2nd Tank Platoon
    - 3rd Tank Platoon
    - 4th Tank Platoon
  - 3rd Tank Company L6/40
    - Command Platoon
    - 1st Tank Platoon
    - 2nd Tank Platoon
    - 3rd Tank Platoon
    - 4th Tank Platoon
  - 4th Motorcycle Company
    - Command Platoon
    - 1st Motorcycle Platoon
    - 2nd Motorcycle Platoon
    - 3rd Motorcycle Platoon
- LXIX Armoured Bersaglieri Battalion
  - Command Company
    - Command Platoon and Connections
  - 5th Company 47/32 L40 self-propelled vehicles
    - Command Platoon
    - 1st Self-Propelled Platoon
    - 2nd Self-Propelled Platoon
  - 6th 20 mm cannon company
    - Command Platoon
    - 1st Platoon
    - 2nd Platoon

- 3rd Platoon
- 4th Platoon

Initially, the 2 battalions were named I Exploring Group and II Exploring Group. A few weeks after its establishment, the two L6/40 tank companies were taken from the staff to form the LXVII Bersaglieri Motorised Battalion, formed on 25 February in Siena, which was later sent to Russia to support the A.R.M.I.R., which was short of armoured elements[12]. The 18th Regiment continued its training without tanks until the end of July, but was, in short order, reinforced with material and personnel from the 5th Bersaglieri Regiment's depot, which went on to reconstitute the Armoured Car Company and the two L6/40 Tank Companies. In November, having moved to Pordenone, the unit was able to complete its tactical and fire training, as well as complete its tank and truck equipment. After being assigned to the 4th Italian Army stationed in Provence on 3 January 1943, the mobilisation order arrived on 8 January and the 18th Bersaglieri Regiment was transferred in stages to France between the 21st and 27th of the same month, deployed in the Toulon hinterland, under the tactical Regiment "Arpens", with garrison and coastal defence duties. The Regiment's units were deployed as follows:

- Arpens Tactical Regiment Command: Brignoles
- Regimental Command: Flessons
- Headquarters and Command Company of the LXVIII Armoured Bersaglieri Battalion: Carnoules
- 1 Armoured car company: Pignans
- 2 L6/40 Tank Company: Pignans
- 3 L6/40 Tank Company: Puget-Ville
- 4 Biker Company: Puget-Ville
- LXIX Armoured Bersaglieri Battalion: Basse.

The L6/40 tanks of the Regiment bore the names of glories and deeds of arms, in which the Regiment had taken part from its establishment until the First World War.
On April 16, 1943, the "Arpens" Tactical Regiment was disbanded and the Regiment passed to the XXII Army Corps, with the artillery support of the CCCLXXII Artillery Group, armed with 149/19 guns. On 10 July, the Armoured Car Company was transferred to the XII Army Corps, becoming the 7th Armoured Car Company, part of the Celere Regiment of occupation in Corsica, as we will see in the next chapter. The 18th Bersaglieri Regiment maintained its positions until the events of 25 July, when, in virtue of the changed political situation and the uncertainty of the evolution of events in Italy, it received the order to return to Italy and relocate to Turin, with public order functions. In early September 1943, the unit began its rail transfer to Lazio, where it would be assigned to the Motorised Army Corps of the 136th Legionary Armoured Division 'Centauro'.

---

12 For an in-depth discussion of the unit's history, see the book 'Italian Armoured Vehicles in Russia 1941-1944' by Paolo Crippa and Antonio Tallillo, Soldiershop, 2022.

224th Coastal Division

It was formed on 1 January 1943 in Florence from reserve units of the Reggimenti Alpini regolari del Regio Esercito (Regular Alpine Regiments of the Royal Army), destined for the coastal defence of the area of Southern France assigned to Italy. It was assigned to the 1st Army Corps and was part of the garrison stationed at Nice.

Although it was not equipped with an armoured component, on 2 January 1943, the 224th Coastal Division was assigned two A.M.D. Panhard 1935 armoured cars (P. Type 178) by the 4th Army Headquarters. These were two cars seized from the French Army following the occupation of Provence (12 - 16 November 1942) and were probably both armed with 2 independent 7.7 mm machine guns in the front turret. The 2 Panhard armoured cars bear the number plates 'RE 1360B' and 'RE 1361B'.

▲ Cover of the magazine 'Signal' depicting the half-sunken battleship 'Strasbourg', occupied by German soldiers.

▲ Italian Cavalry units at a location on the Côte d'Azur.

▼ The cruiser 'Colbert' sank starboard after being set on fire in the port of Toulon. The COLBERT, which was set on fire, also sank starboard. The battleship 'Strasbourg' is seen behind.

▲ Officers of the 48th Alpine Artillery Regiment in Cuers, a town not far from Toulon, in December 1942 (WEB source).

▲ Official ceremony of the 48th Alpine Artillery Regiment in Cuers on 4 December 1942 (WEB source).

▼ L6/40 tanks of the Piedmont Royal Cavalry Regiment enter Nice in the autumn of 1942 (Benvenuti - Colonna).

▲ The population of Nice observes with concern the arrival of Italian armoured troops in the city (Benvenuti - Colonna).

▼ Another image of the L6/40 light tank column marching through the streets of Nice (Benvenuti - Colonna).

▲ Close-up of one of the L6/40 tanks in Nice (Benvenuti - Colonna).

▼ Italian tanks in motion in a square in the city of Nice, during the Italian occupation in the autumn of 1942 (Benvenuti - Colonna).

▲ The column of L6/40 tanks marching along the famous Promenade des Anglais, one of the symbols of the city of Nice.

▼ Italian tanks photographed from another perspective on the Promenade des Anglais (Benvenuti - Colonna).

▲ A Royal Army mover directs traffic in Nice in the autumn of 1942 (B.A.).

▼ German soldiers photographed in Monte Carlo on the terrace of the Casino. The town had been occupied by Italian troops in the autumn of 1942, like other locations on the Côte d'Azur (private collection).

▲ The Army Corps Commander reviews the motorbike and tank units (Benvenuti - Colonna).

▼ The armoured vehicles parade in front of the Army Corps Commander, filmed by a military cameraman (Benvenuti - Colonna).

OCCUPATION OF CORSICA (NOVEMBER 1942 – SEPTEMBER 1943)

Corsica had been occupied by the Italians in November 1942 and at the time of the Armistice, the VII Army Corps, commanded by General Magli, was manned by some 60,900 soldiers. The Italian Headquarters in Corsica were located at the Hotel 'de la Paix' in Corte, a village with a fortified citadel in the north-central mountains of the island.

The one in Corsica was the only victorious resistance on French territory; the following armoured units were present on the island:

- CXXXI Battalion Semoventi from 47/32
- XX Self-propelled Battalion 47/32
- XIII Tank Battalion L
- I Tank Battalion L
- II Tank Battalion L
- 10th Celere Regiment

A total of 55 L40 47/32 self-propelled vehicles, 69 L3/35 and L3/38 light tanks and 17 AB41 armoured cars were available on the island.

In the second half of 1943, the Italian commands had to deal with a growing feeling of hostility on the French side. The ratio of the Italian contingent to the island's inhabitants was almost exaggerated, with a ratio of about one soldier for every three inhabitants, a situation that was experienced by the Corsicans as a kind of constant provocation. The Italian authorities tried in every way to give the military presence a purely defensive character against possible Allied attacks, but the Corsicans increasingly perceived it as a real occupation as time went on.

The Italian units, unaware of the Armistice, were garrisoning long stretches of coastline on 8 September to avoid Allied landings, while the Germans of the SS-Sturmbrigade 'Reichsführer SS' were stationed in the Sartene area. In support of the latter, on the night between 8 and 9 September, the 90th Panzergrenadier-Division landed in Bonifacio and immediately the Italian units were engaged by the now former Allies, with lightning actions aimed at the complete occupation of the island. The surprise caused by the German attack greatly disoriented the Italian divisions, initially convinced that they were being attacked by American troops, but once the situation became clear, the Italian reaction proved decisive and inflicted heavy losses on the Germans. It should be noted, however, that General Giovanni Magli, the island's military commander, received information of the Armistice about an hour before Badoglio's announcement on Radio London and prepared to resist the inevitable German reaction by freeing French partisans captured in the previous months. Around 1 a.m. there were the first contacts between the Italians and the Germans, who attempted to occupy the port of Bastia. The German attack was successful and the port was immediately lost, but the Royal Army units managed to regain possession in a short time. The occupation of the harbour would have been a great advantage for the Germans: on the one hand it would have precluded the Italian troops from re-entering Sardinia, on the other hand they would have ensured safe access to receive reinforcements and supplies. The clashes involved the self-propelled vehicles of the XX Self-propelled 47/32 Battalion of the 'Friuli' Division, which was stationed in the town, L3 tanks and some AB41s. Almost at the same time, violent clashes broke out in many parts of the island, with mixed fortunes, and the port of Bastia was once again lost. In fact, the Italians managed for a few days to fend off new attempts to occupy the port by the German armed forces, but, on 13 September, with the support of Tiger tanks, the Germans got the better of them and the Italians were forced to retreat and hide while waiting for Allied support.

On the 14th of September, the 4th Franco-Moroccan Division of the 1st Army Corps began to arrive in the port of Ajaccio, in support of the Italian troops, and on the 23rd, the 1st Battery of the DLXI Self-propelled Group of 75/18, with 6 pieces, arrived in Ajaccio from Sardinia; the Battery was then moved to Corte, participating in the subsequent operations against the Germans, reaching as far as Bastia. From that moment, after the Degollists had made contact with General Magli, the operations on the Bastia front continued jointly and the collaboration between the Italians and the French led to the complete defeat of the German troops between 29 September and 4 October. On that day, the vital port of Bastia was once again recaptured by units of the Bersaglieri, the 4th Mechanized Regiment and the Goumiers of the 1st Moroccan Regiment, supported by L40 self-propelled vehicles. The German forces were thus forced to embark for safety on the mainland, and the following day the last German prisoners were captured.

The immediate reaction and compactness with which the Italian units reacted to the German offensive meant that the island did not witness the terrible rout that took place in the Balkans, despite the fact that the fighting was sustained by the Italian units in a clearly inferior state of armament. However, the efforts made allowed the French troops to land undisturbed and the combativeness of the Italian soldiers inflicted significant losses on the Germans, causing them to abandon the island.

After eliminating the German threat on the island, however, the Allied commands no longer deemed the presence of Italian armoured units advisable, so much so that the units present in Sardinia were confiscated materials, such as tank radio stations, in order to make them unusable, while those stationed in Corsica had to surrender their armoured vehicles to the Degollists and the Italian soldiers were treated almost like prisoners of war. All self-propelled vehicles were confiscated from the CLXXXI and XX Battalion by the French units and the two units were transferred to Sardinia (on 20 October the XX Battalion and the following day the CLXXXI), only to be transferred to the Peninsula at the end of the year, being transformed into simple framework battalions. On 17 October, the 13th Tank Battalion L had landed in Palau, where it was disbanded the following month, with the exception of the Motorized Gunner Company, which remained autonomous, and on 22 October, the 1st Battery of the DLXI Self-propelled 75/18 Group returned to its unit in Sardinia[13].

---

13 The Battery had to surrender 7 CL39 trucks, 4 Benelli two-seater motorbikes and a FIAT 1100 car to the French units.

The Italian blood toll in the fighting in Corsica was high, over 600 killed, who today rest in the 'Lupi di Toscana' cemetery in Livorno. During the operations in Corsica, Captain Giovanni Carta, Second Lieutenant Giuseppe Giuliano, Sergeant Ettore Moretti (in memory) and Carristi Bernardino Cenni and Pietro Zanni of the CXXXI Battaglione Semoventi da 47/32 were decorated with the Bronze Medal for Military Valour, while Second Lieutenant Domenico Chicco, the battalion's medical officer, was awarded the Military Cross for Military Valour.

Even today, almost 80 years after the end of World War II, it is easy to come across remnants of the conflict in Corsica, especially motor vehicles and armoured vehicles, some of which, especially in recent years, have been the subject of recovery and museumisation projects. The most famous recovery and restoration is probably that of a 47/32 self-propelled vehicle, which had belonged to the 'Cremona' Division. This self-propelled vehicle, along with other vehicles abandoned by the Italians, was used in the post-war period as a tractor by a woodcutter, who abandoned it in the mountains after the first breakdown. The armoured vehicle was found in 2008, on the recommendation of its former owner, on the plateau between Livio and Conca; it was subsequently the subject of a two-year restoration carried out by Jean-Noël Aiquied and is now kept at the Musée de la Résistance Corse in Zonza. Although the restoration was not carried out in a philologically correct manner and the vehicle has many reconstruction errors, it is the only 47/32 L40 self-propelled gun preserved in the world, apart from the one in Aberdeen in the United States, at the US Army Ordnance Museum.

Armoured Units

CXXXI Battalion Semoventi da 47/32 of Infantry Division 'Cremona'
It came from the Depot of the 31st Carristi Regiment in Siena, formed out of 2 Self-propelled Platoons. Assigned to the Infantry Division 'Cremona', the Battalion was sent to Corsica in November 1942 following the Allied landings in Algeria and Tunisia.

XX Self-propelled 47/32 Battalion of the 'Friuli' Infantry Division
The Battalion had been formed at the Verona Depot of the 32nd Carristi Regiment, where it had been formed in October 1942, on 2 Platoons of L40 47/32 Semoventi L40s. It was commanded by Lieutenant Colonel Alessandro Minelli and was assigned to the 'Friuli' Division, to be sent to Corsica at the end of the same month of October.

I Tank Battalion L of the 33rd Tank Regiment
The unit was commanded by Major Gaspare Calcara, came from the 33rd Carristi Regiment's depot, equipped exclusively with L3/35 and some L6/40 tanks, and was organised on:
- Command Company (with 2 L3/35 and 2 L6/40 tanks)
- 1st Company (with 13 L3/35 tanks)
- 2nd Company (with 13 L3/35 tanks)

- 3rd Company (with 13 L3/35 tanks)

II Tank Battalion L of the 33rd Tank Regiment
The unit came from the depot of the 33rd Tank Regiment, which was equipped exclusively with L3/35 tanks.

XIII Tank Battalion L of the 33rd Tank Regiment
The Battalion came from the 33rd Carristi Regiment, under the command of Major Antonio Anedda, and was largely equipped with L3 light tanks upgraded to standard 38. The Battalion, stationed in Sardinia, had been sent to Corsica during the occupation of the island in November 1942 and had a staff of 22 officers, 32 non-commissioned officers and 316 troops and was made up of:
- Command Company
- 1st Tank Company
- 2nd Tank Company
- Motor Gunnery Company

10th Celere Regiment
This Regiment, under the command of Lieutenant Colonel Ettore Fucci, was made up of Battalions and Companies detached from Depots and Regiments, to be placed at the disposal of VII Corps in Corsica. The Regiment was formed in Corte, where the Italian Command of Corsica was located; composed of Alpini and Bersaglieri it was a sort of rapid intervention force, to be used for any eventuality in any part of the island; its main tasks were patrolling the communication routes, to prevent partisan attacks on convoys and road sabotage, and coastal defence. The Regiment was made up of:
- Command
- XXXIII Bersaglieri Cyclist Battalion[14]
- LXXI Motorised Bersaglieri Battalion
- 107th Motorcycle Company
- 7th Armoured Car Company, on Command Platoon and 4 Armoured Car Platoons, with 17 AB41 armoured cars

The latter Company was none other than the 1st Company of the 18th Bersaglieri Regiment, which had been detached from the original unit and sent to the Lane as reinforcement for the 10th Celere Regiment.

---

14 It was located in Vizzavona, a tiny village about 40 kilometres south of Corte, at an altitude of 900 metres.

▲ Landing of self-propelled 47/32s in the port of Bastia on 11 November 1942.

▼ Another 47/32 self-propelled vehicle of the CXXXI Battalion L40 self-propelled vehicles landed in Bastia. It is a self-propelled Platoon Commander, from the 1st Platoon of the 2nd Company.

▲ Another image of the CXXXI Battalion's L40 self-propelled vehicles, concentrated on the docks of the port of Bastia in the autumn of 1942.

▼ A section of Blackshirts just landed in Corsica in the port of Bastia.

▲ Black Shirts marching in a Corsican town: interesting the use of the 'Samurai' magazine carrier by the legionnaire on the far right, who, consequently, must have been armed with a MAB 38 automatic musket.

▼ Italian L3 tanks on the Ajaccio waterfront in Corsica (Benvenuti - Colonna).

▲ An officer of the Voluntary National Security Militia unit, pictured in the previous photograph, conferring with a French gendarme.

▲ On the Place d'Austerlitz in Ajaccio, in front of the monument dedicated to Napoleon Bonaparte, parade some Italian L3/33 tanks of the XIII Tank Battalion L: these are two command tanks, equipped with radio equipment (Benvenuti - Colonna).

▼ Close-up of one of the two tanks in the previous photo: it is entirely painted in dark green (Manes).

▲ Another L3/33 of the XIII Tank Battalion L near the monument to Napoleon in Ajaccio (Benvenuti - Colonna).

▼ Italian armoured cars at Court in Corsica.

▲ Italian armoured cars of the 7th Bersaglieri Regiment in Avenue Jean Nicoli in Corte, north-central Corsica, the town where the Italian Command post on the island was located, in November 1942.

▼ Some Bersaglieri of the Celere Regiment at a road crossroads in northern Corsica.

▲ An artillery unit takes up position in Corsican territory during the Italian occupation. A FIAT 508 Cm car can be seen in the foreground, behind it a TL37 tractor.

▼ An AB41 on the move on an impassable road in northern Corsica.

▲ Column consisting of three AB41 armoured cars of the 10th Celere Regiment and SPA 38 trucks.

▼ AB41 armoured cars photographed in Corsica on 6 November 1942, shortly after their arrival on the island.

▲ AB41 armoured car of the Bersaglieri of the 7th Armoured Car Company of the 10th Celere Regiment marching near the built-up area of Corte, whose historic centre can be seen in the background on the right.

▲ Italian artillerymen army the use of captured French heavy coast artillery.
▼ A column of Italian trucks moves along a carriageway: in the background you can see the snow-capped Monte Cinto.

▲ AB41 armoured cars patrol a road at high altitude: the presence of Italian soldiers in Corsica was, in relation to the population, extremely high.

▼ A column of TL37s with guns in tow goes into position for an exercise.

▲ The guns are detached from the tractors and put into position.

▼ Camouflaged position of one of the 75/27 guns on the heights of Corsica, belonging to the unit photographed in the previous pictures.

▲ A motorcyclist and a tank driver from an Italian armoured division photographed in front of a tobacco shop.

▼ Armoured men and motorcyclists of the Bersaglieri of the 10th Celere Regiment escort a column through the streets of a town in Corsica, near an Italian checkpoint, which was reinforced with roadblocks made of dry stone walls.

▲ L40 self-propelled vehicles on the move: the first one is marked 'RE 4237'.

▼ An armoured car patrol of the 10th Celere Regiment leaves the town of Corte: the cars have snow chains on their bows, which are also used on muddy ground to increase tyre grip.

▲ The AB41s, on which branches were placed for camouflage purposes, filmed from another angle.

▼ Wehrmacht officers in conversation during embarkation for Corsica in Palau on 8 September 1943 (B.A.).

▲ German vehicles of the 90.Panzergrenadier-Division departed from Sardinia, where they were to accompany the soldiers of the SS-Sturmbrigade 'Reichsführer SS', with the aim of overthrowing the Italian armed forces and taking over the island (B.A.).

▼ German soldiers of the 90.Panzergrenadier-Division while sailing towards Corsica.

▲ The island of Corsica is in sight and the tankers of the 90.Panzergrenadier-Division prepare to land.

▼ A Carrista officer scans the horizon with binoculars from an L3/33 Radio in Corsica; one can see how the tank has been brought up to CV38 standards by the presence of battery boxes on the front mudguards (Arena).

▲ CV38 tanks in Corsica parked in front of a school. The first tank, an L3/38 Radio with stylus antenna, bears the metallic crest of the Carristi on the front of the tank and has reddish-brown and black camouflage and spots on a green background (Arena).

▼ Holy Mass in the field officiated among the 47/32 self-propelled vehicles in Corsica (Crippa).

▲ A column of CXXXI Battalion L40 self-propelled vehicles marching through the Corsican heights.

▼ The same column as in the previous photo passes through a built-up area. The vehicle in the lead is a command vehicle, equipped with radio equipment; all self-propelled vehicles have a uniform sand-yellow colour scheme.

▲ Stu.G. III self-propelled vehicles of the SS-Sturmbrigade 'Reichsführer SS' moved from Bastia towards the ports of San Bonifacio and Porto Vecchio, where the units of the 90. Panzergrenadier-Division (Arena) were to land.

▲ A unit of Bersaglieri motorcyclists from the 10th Celere Regiment, supported by an AB41 armoured car, parked in a village in Corsica.

▼ AB41 crews in a break during a transfer.

▲ Stu.G. III self-propelled vehicles of the SS-Sturmbrigade 'Reichsführer SS' stopped awaiting orders after the Armistice announcement.

▲ Group photo of German soldiers of the SS-Sturmbrigade 'Reichsführer SS', portrayed during a break.

▼ Italian health soldiers on the move in a Corsican village during sustained fighting against German troops.

▲ Self-propelled Stu.G. III of the SS-Sturmbrigade 'Reichsführer SS' on the march.

▼ Close-up of the crew of a Stu.G. III of the SS-Sturmbrigade 'Reichsführer SS'.

▲ The support of Italian L40 self-propelled vehicles in the battles against the Germans in the days following the Armistice was crucial: in this picture, one of these vehicles, camouflaged with branches, moving along a country road.

▼ A 47/32 L40 self-propelled command vehicle of the CXXXI Battalion Semoventi L40: the image allows us to appreciate the sandy yellow colouring and the presence of the antenna, indicative of the presence of the radio linking apparatus. On the far left, another similar vehicle can be seen.

▲ Italian armoured vehicles garrison the Boulevard Dominique Paoli in Bastia after the Armistice announcement.

▼ A 47/32 L40 self-propelled vehicle of the XX Battalion Semoventi da 47/32 guards the port of Bastia in Corsica, after the Italian troops had recaptured it from the German military; the vehicle has the number plate 'RE 5720'; in the background the damaged steamer 'Humanitas' (Arena).

▲ After a night of fighting, the port of Bastia, occupied by the German troops for only a few hours, was retaken thanks to decisive Italian intervention, supported by the self-propelled units of the 20th Battalion.

▲ Along the road to Bastia, the wreck of a German Stug. III Ausf. G of the SS-Sturmbrigade 'Reichsführer SS', destroyed by Italian artillery, is inspected by soldiers of the Royal Army (Arena).

▼ A refurbished (with some poetic licence) L40 47/32 Semovente L40 is kept at the Musée de la Résistance Corse in Zonza, a village on the Alta Rocca in Corsica.

▲ A French officer of the forces loyal to De Gaulle studies a map together with an officer of the 20th Battalion Semoventi and one of the 'Friuli' Division in Corsica.

BIBLIOGRAPHY

Books
- AA.VV., "Storia dei mezzi corazzati", Fratelli Fabbri Editori, Milano 1976.
- AA.VV., "Giugno 1940 - Guerra sulle Alpi", Italia Editrice, Campobasso, 1994.
- AA.VV., "Soldati e Battaglie della Seconda Guerra Mondiale", Hobby & Work Italiana Editrice, Bresso (MI), 1999.
- Barba Selene, "La Resistenza dei militari italiani all'Estero – Francia e Corsica", Rivista militare, Roma, 1995.
- Barlozzetti Ugo, Pirella Alberto, "Mezzi dell'Esercito italiano 1935 – 1945", Editoriale Olimpia, Firenze, 1986.
- Benvenuti Bruno, Colonna Ugo, "Fronte Terra" volumi 1, 2/I, 2/II e 2/III, Edizioni Bizzarri, Roma 1974.
- Cappellano Filippo, Pignato Nicola, "Gli autoveicoli da combattimento dell'Esercito Italiano", volume I, S.M.E. – Ufficio Storico, Roma, 2002.
- Cappellano Filippo, Pignato Nicola, "Gli autoveicoli da combattimento dell'Esercito Italiano", volume II, S.M.E. – Ufficio Storico, Roma, 2002.
- Cappellano Filippo, Pignato Nicola, "Il Regio Esercito alla vigilia dell'8 settembre 1943", Ermanno Albertelli Editore Parma, 2003.
- Carloni Fabrizio, "L'occupazione italiana della Corsica – novembre 1942 – ottobre 1943", Mursia, Milano, 2016.
- Ceva Lucio, Curami Andrea, "La meccanizzazione dell'Esercito fino al 1943", S.M.E – Ufficio Storico, Roma, 1989.
- Commissione Italiana di Storia Militare, "La partecipazione delle Forze Armate alla Guerra di Liberazione e di Resistenza – 8 settembre 1943 8 maggio 1945", Ente Editoriale per l'Anna dei Carabinieri, Roma, 2003.
- Corbatti Sergio, Nava Marco, "Come il diamante", Laran Editions, Bruxelles, 2008.
- Crippa Paolo, Manes Luigi, "Italia 43-45 - I mezzi delle Unità cobelligeranti", Mattioli 1885, Fidenza (PR), 2018.
- De Lorenzis Ugo, "Dal primo all'ultimo giorno. Ricordi di guerra 1939 - 1945", Longanesi, Milano, 1971.
- Guglielmi Daniele, Tallillo Andrea, Tallillo Antonio, "Carro L3. Carri veloci, carri leggeri, derivati", GMT, Trento, 2004.
- Guglielmi Daniele, Tallillo Andrea, Tallillo Antonio, "Carro L6 – Carri leggeri, semoventi, derivati", seconda edizione, GMT, Trento, 2019.
- Guglielmi Daniele, Tallillo Andrea, Tallillo Antonio, "Carro M. Carri medi M11/39, M13/40, M14/41, M15/42, semoventi e altri derivati", GMT, Trento, 2010.
- Guglielmi Daniele, Tallillo Andrea, Tallillo Antonio, "Carro M. Carri medi M11/39, M13/40, M14/41, M15/42, semoventi e altri derivati", volume 2, GMT, Trento, 2012.
- Masacci Luca, "I veicoli corazzati italiani 1940 – 1943: album fotografico", Mattioli 1885, Fidenza (PR), 2013.
- Mattesini Francesco, "La guerra con la Francia – Le operazioni aeronavali italiane e francesi nel mediterraneo occidentale e l'offensiva della 4 Armata italiana nelle Alpi – 11 – 25 giugno

- 1940", Soldiershop, Zanica (BG), 2023.
- Panicacci Jean-Louis, "L'occupazione italiana del Nizzardo. Operazione strategica e irredentista (giugno 1940-settembre 1943)", Fusta, Saluzzo (CN), 2017.
- Papò Paolo Emilio, "I mezzi corazzati italiani. I primi quarant'anni", IBN Editore, Roma, 2011.
- Papò Paolo Emilio, "Armistizio!", IBN Editore, Roma, 2020.
- Parri Maurizio, "Tracce di Cingolo", A.N.C.I., Verona, 2016.
- Parri Maurizio e Bianchi Carlo, "A Nessuno Secondi, le ricompense al valor militare ai Carristi dal 1927 a oggi", A.N.C.I., Roma, 2020.
- Pignato Nicola, "1912 – 1985 Dalla Libia al Libano", Editrice Scorpione, Taranto, 1989.
- Pignato Nicola, "Motori!!! Le truppe corazzate italiane 1919 – 1994", GMT, Trento, 1995.
- Pignato Nicola, "Italian Armored Vehicles of World War Two", Squadron Signal Publications, USA, 2004.
- Pignato Nicola, "Italian Medium Tank in Action", Squadron Signal Piblications, USA, 2001.
- Pignato Nicola, Cappella Filippo, "Insegne, uniformi, distintivi e tradizioni delle truppe corazzate italiane", T&T Editore, Dogana (San Marino), 2005.
- Pignato Nicola, "Un secolo di autoblindate in Italia", Mattioli 1885, Fidenza (PR), 2008.
- Riccio Ralph A., "Italian tanks and combat vehicles of World War II", Mattioli 1885, Fidenza (PR), 2010.
- Romeo Pierluigi di Colloredo Mels, "Giugno 1940 – La battaglia delle Alpi", Soldiershop, Zanica (BG), 2020.
- Schipsi Domenico, "L'occupazione italiana dei territori metropolitani francesi 1940 – 1943", Ufficio Storico dello Stato Maggiore dell'Esercito, Roma, 2007.

Articles
- Corino Giorgio, "Diario di un sergente della Fanteria Carrista", in "Il Carrista d'Italia", numero 318, gennaio/febbraio/marzo 2024.
- Galantini Cesare, "La battaglia della Corsica", in "Resistenza e antifascismo oggi", anno XXIII, numero 2, aprile 2012.

Magazines
- "Il Carrista d'Italia", organo dell'Associazione Nazionale Carristi d'Italia, numeri vari.
- "Rivista Militare", numeri vari.
- "Storia Militare", numeri vari.
- "Bastie – La Ville magazine", numero 41, "70eme anniversaire de la Libération de la Corse – Septembre – Octobre 1943: la Ville se souvient", novembre 2013, Bastia (Francia).

Other publications
- AA.VV., "L'Esercito Italiano nella guerra di Liberazione", supplemento a "Rivista Militare n°1, Stato Maggiore dell'Esercito - Ufficio Generale Promozione, Pubblicistica e Storia, Roma 2020.
- Cervi Oliviero, "Il II/33°, mio battaglione", gennaio 1984, memoria dattiloscritta, copia fotostatica in possesso dell'autore.

TITOLI GIÀ PUBBLICATI - TITLES ALREADY PUBLISHING

BOOKS TO COLLECT

www.ingramcontent.com/pod-product-compliance
Lightning Source LLC
LaVergne TN
LVHW081451060526
838201LV00050BA/1769